Pathways to Artistry

A Method for Comprehensive Technical and Musical Development

Catherine Rollin

3

MASTERWORKS

The goal of the *Pathways to Artistry* series is to emphasize the importance of technique and artistry beginning at the early stages of piano study. The pieces in *Masterworks*, Book 3 represent some of the best early intermediate masterworks in the piano literature. For the maximum benefit, students should work through the skills that are comprehensively described in *Pathways to Artistry Technique*, Book 3. (See page 48 for a summary of these skills.)

In addition to standard editing, I have included "physical vocabulary" indications based on specific skills developed in *Pathways to Artistry Technique*, Books 1, 2, and 3. As with any editorial input, the physical vocabulary indicated is only provided as a guideline. **The most important learning experience for students is becoming aware of how using a physical vocabulary affects the ultimate artistic result.** To further students' musical growth, each piece includes a music history timeline, a brief composer biography and labels for form.

Good technique and musical artistry are inseparable. Their mastery is often a lifetime quest. It is my hope that through this series, students will find themselves on the pathway to that goal.

Alfred Music Publishing Co., Inc.
P.O. Box 10003
Van Nuys, CA 91410-0003
alfred.com

Copyright © MMIX by Alfred Music Publishing Co., Inc.
All rights reserved. Printed in USA.

ISBN-10: 0-7390-6494-0
ISBN-13: 978-0-7390-6494-8

Cover Photo: Pierre-Yves Goavec/Getty Images

MW00782694

Contents

Menuet en Rondeau

This piece is from the

Jean-Philippe Rameau was a well known French composer, harpsichordist, organist, and music theorist. His famous *Treatise on Harmony* has influenced the study of music theory since it was written in the 18th century.

Baroque Era
ca. 1600–1750

Classical Era
ca. 1750–1820

Romantic Era
ca. 1790–1910

Contemporary Era
ca. 1900–present

Jean-Philippe Rameau
(1683–1764)

Écossaise in G Major

This piece is from the

Franz Schubert was a great Austrian composer. Known for his beautiful melodies, he wrote in both Classical and Romantic styles. This piece is representative of his Classical works.

Baroque Era ca. 1600–1750	Classical Era ca. 1750–1820	Romantic Era ca. 1790–1910	Contemporary Era ca. 1900–present

A Section
Allegretto

Franz Schubert
(1797–1828)

*fz is the abbreviation for forzando, which means accented.

German Dance in D Major

This piece is from the

Franz Joseph Haydn was born in Austria. He was one of the most influential composers of the Classical era. He also had the distinction of being one of Beethoven's teachers. Beethoven dedicated his first piano sonata to Haydn.

| Baroque Era ca. 1600–1750 | Classical Era ca. 1750–1820 | Romantic Era ca. 1790–1910 | Contemporary Era ca. 1900–present |

Arabesque
Op. 100, No, 2
This piece is from the

Johann Friedrich Burgmüller was a German pianist and composer. He moved to Paris in 1832 and was influenced by Parisian salon music. His pedagogical pieces are among the most popular in the piano repertoire.

| Baroque Era ca. 1600–1750 | Classical Era ca. 1750–1820 | Romantic Era ca. 1790–1910 | Contemporary Era ca. 1900–present |

Johann Friedrich Burgmüller
(1806–1874)

*The short portatos on the quarter notes wil create a pulse in the arm like an internal metronome. Maintain this same pulse when moving from the A section to the B section.

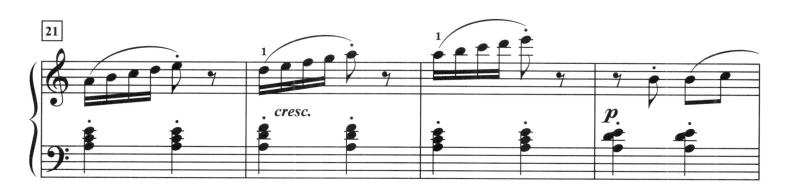

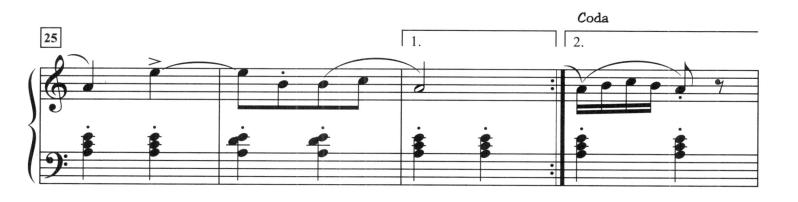

Écossaise in G Major

This piece is from the

Ludwig van Beethoven was a German composer. He is considered by many to be one of the greatest musical geniuses in history. While much of his music is very serious, many of his pieces, such as this écossaise, reflect his great humor and wit.

| Baroque Era ca. 1600–1750 | Classical Era ca. 1750–1820 | Romantic Era ca. 1790–1910 | Contemporary Era ca. 1900–present |

Ludwig van Beethoven
(1770–1827)

Etude in A Minor

This piece is from the

Cornelius Gurlitt was a German organist, pianist, and composer. He produced a prolific amount of pedagogical piano works. His piano miniatures are reminiscent of the character pieces of Robert Schumann.

Baroque Era ca. 1600–1750	Classical Era ca. 1750–1820	Romantic Era ca. 1790–1910	Contemporary Era ca. 1900–present

Cornelius Gurlitt
(1820–1901)

Minuet in G Major
from the *Notebook for Anna Magdalena Bach*

This piece is from the

Christian Petzold was a German composer. For many years, the Menuet in G Major was attributed to J. S. Bach. Recent research has led scholars to conclude that Petzold was the composer of this famous menuet.

| Baroque Era ca. 1600–1750 | Classical Era ca. 1750–1820 | Romantic Era ca. 1790–1910 | Contemporary Era ca. 1900–present |

Christian Petzold
(1677–1733)

B Section

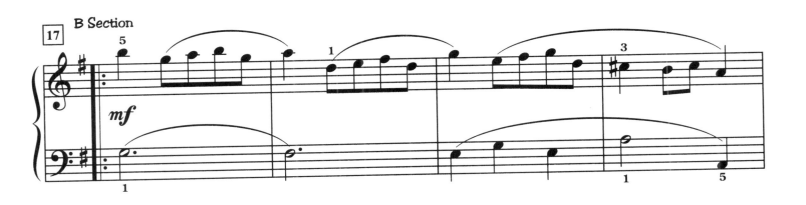

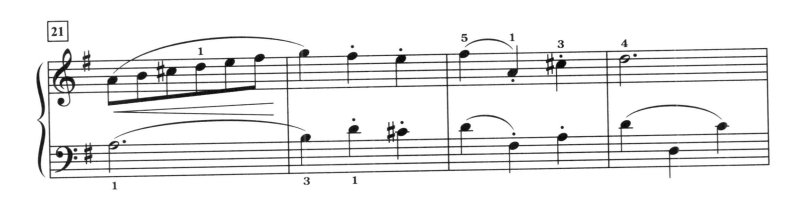

dim. e poco rit. last time

tenuto last time

* Optional: Play as a rolled chord the last time.

Écossaise in C Major

This piece is from the

Johann Nepomuk Hummel was an Austrian composer, pianist, and teacher. He was highly lauded in his lifetime and even compared by critics to Beethoven. He wrote many works for piano, including several excellent pedagogical pieces.

Baroque Era	Classical Era	Romantic Era	Contemporary Era
ca. 1600–1750	ca. 1750–1820	ca. 1790–1910	ca. 1900–present

Johann Nepomuk Hummel
(1778–1837)

*Students with small hands may omit the low F on beat 1 and the F on beat 2 in measures 3 and 7.
**Play the grace note quickly on the beat.

Summer Journey

This piece is from the

Anatoli Liadov was a Russian composer. He was very interested in Russian folk music and fairy tales. He was one of the influential composers of the early 20th century in Russia. His most-famous student was Sergei Prokofiev.

| Baroque Era ca. 1600–1750 | Classical Era ca. 1750–1820 | Romantic Era ca. 1790–1910 | Contemporary Era ca. 1900–present |

Section A

Andante con moto

Anatoli Liadov
(1855–1914)

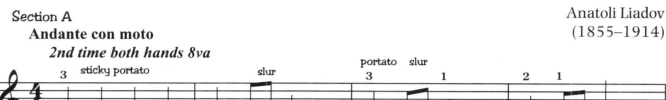

LH legato through compass pivots

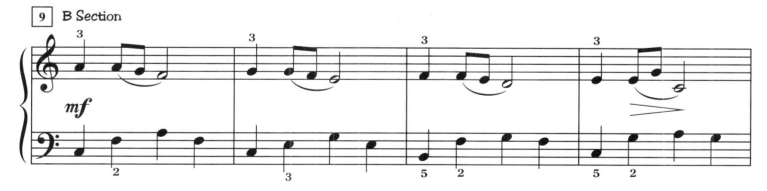

Bagatelle
Op. 125, No. 10

This piece is from the

Anton Diabelli was an Austrian composer, publisher, and musician. He was active as a piano and guitar teacher and also published the music of the great Franz Schubert.

Baroque Era ca. 1600–1750	Classical Era ca. 1750–1820	Romantic Era ca. 1790–1910	Contemporary Era ca. 1900–present

A Section
Allegretto

Anton Diabelli
(1781–1858)

* Play the grace note quickly on the beat.

B Section

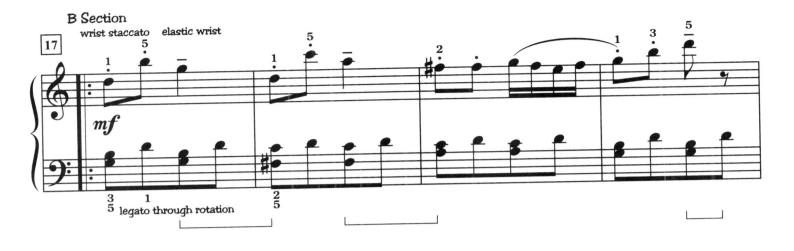

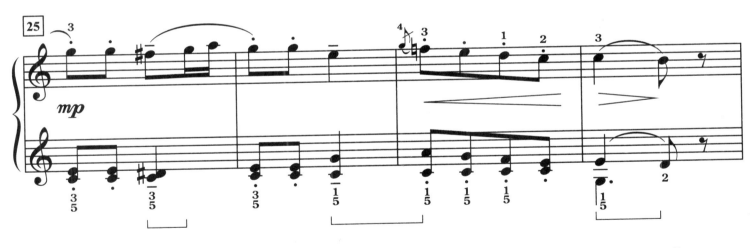

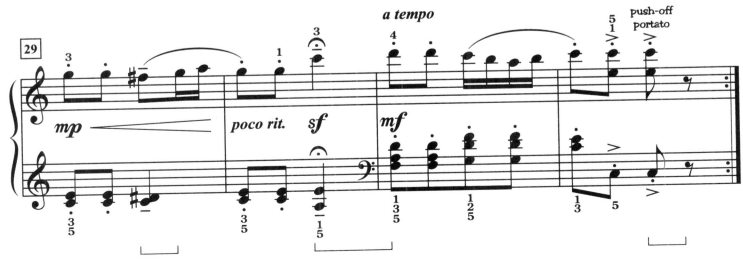

Theme and Variation in G Major

This piece is from the

Cornelius Gurlitt was one of the most successful pedagogical composers to emerge from the Romantic era. While his works truly capture the drama of the Romantic spirit, they lie comfortably in the hands of developing pianists.

| Baroque Era ca. 1600–1750 | Classical Era ca. 1750–1820 | Romantic Era ca. 1790–1910 | Contemporary Era ca. 1900–present |

Cornelius Gurlitt
(1820–1901)

A Section
Andante cantabile

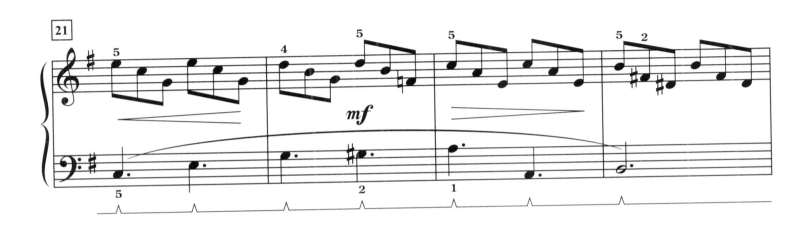

Hey, tulip, tulip
from *For Children*

This piece is from the

Béla Bartók was a great Hungarian composer. He was also an outstanding pianist. His compositions were often influenced by the folk music of numerous countries including his native Hungary as well Rumania and Bulgaria.

Baroque Era	Classical Era	Romantic Era	Contemporary Era
ca. 1600–1750	ca. 1750–1820	ca. 1790–1910	ca. 1900–present

Béla Bartók
(1881–1945)

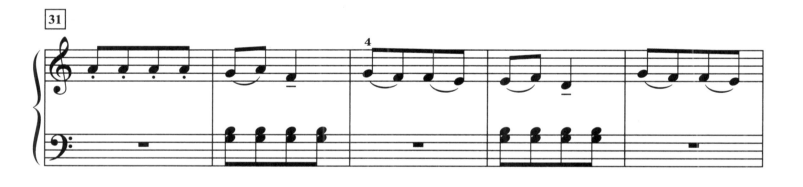

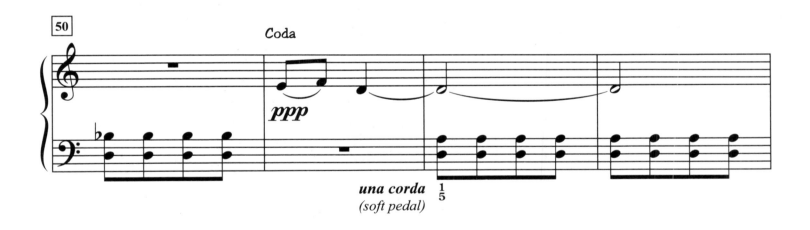

Musette in G Major

Johann Sebastian Bach was a German composer and one of the most brilliant and influential musicians in history. His work is considered to be the apex of the Baroque era.

This piece is from the

Baroque Era
ca. 1600–1750

Classical Era
ca. 1750–1820

Romantic Era
ca. 1790–1910

Contemporary Era
ca. 1900–present

Johann Sebastian Bach
(1685–1750)

* Hold finger 5 and shift weight to the fingers that are playing.

Minuet in F Major

K. 6

This piece is from the

Wolfgang Amadeus Mozart was born in Austria. He was probably the greatest musical prodigy in history. In his short life, he produced a large body of work including piano and violin sonatas, concertos and many symphonies and operas.

Baroque Era	Classical Era	Romantic Era	Contemporary Era
ca. 1600–1750	ca. 1750–1820	ca. 1790–1910	ca. 1900–present

Wolfgang Amadeus Mozart
(1756–1791)

alternating hand technique
sticky portato (both hands)

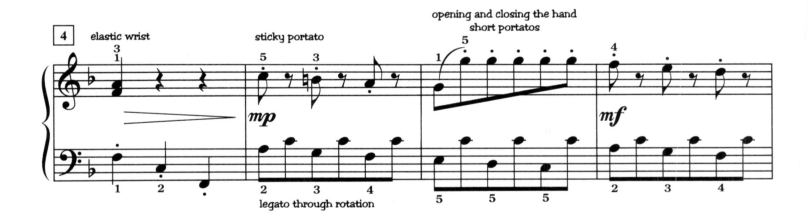

23

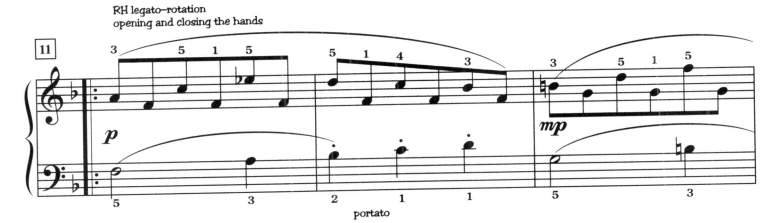

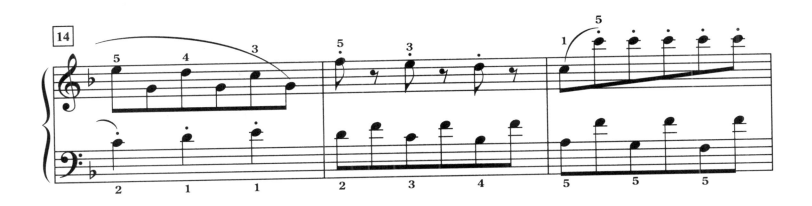

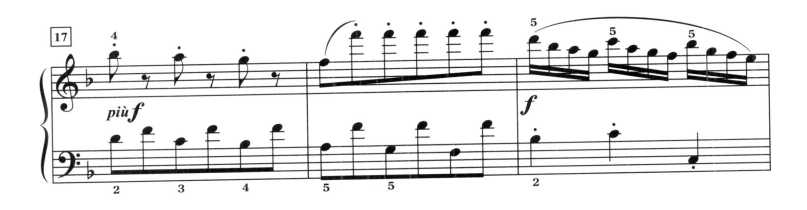

Distant Bells
Op. 63, No. 6

This piece is from the

Jean Louis Streabbog was a French composer and pianist. Many of his delightful teaching pieces have been student favorites for over a century.

Baroque Era ca. 1600–1750	Classical Era ca. 1750–1820	Romantic Era ca. 1790–1910	Contemporary Era ca. 1900–present

A Section
Andante

Jean Louis Streabbog
(1835–1886)

* The wedge accent indicates emphasis on the note. On the half note, use portato with a little extra arm weight to create the sound of bells. The pedal will sustain the ringing sound.

25

Sonatina in C Major
Op. 39, No. 1 (First Movement)

This piece is from the

Frank Lynes was an American composer and teacher. He is best known for the piano sonatinas that he wrote for students. Although he lived in the Romantic era, he was influenced by the Classical style of Kuhlau and Clementi.

Baroque Era	Classical Era	Romantic Era	Contemporary Era
ca. 1600–1750	ca. 1750–1820	ca. 1790–1910	ca. 1900–present

Exposition
A Theme
Allegro

Frank Lynes
(1858–1913)

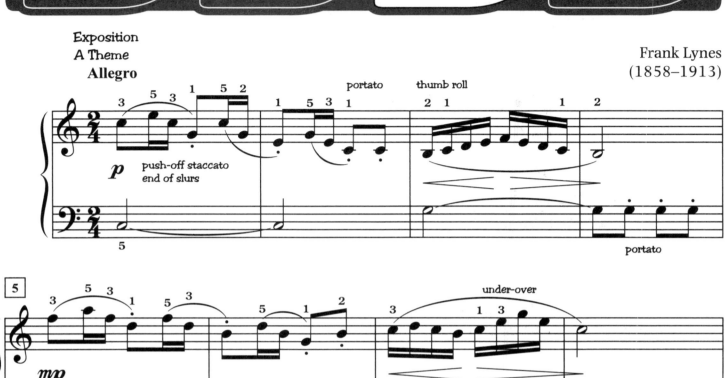

B Theme

LH legato

Development (transition)

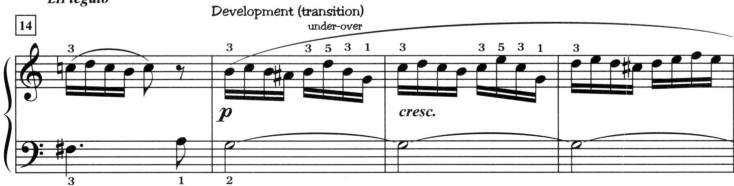

Two Character Pieces

These pieces are from the

Cornelius Gurlitt was the master of character pieces that also were excellent pedagogically. His compositions have very distinctive personalities that help develop the interpretive skills of students.

| Baroque Era ca. 1600–1750 | Classical Era ca. 1750–1820 | Romantic Era ca. 1790–1910 | Contemporary Era ca. 1900–present |

Storm at Sea

Cornelius Gurlitt (1820–1901)
Op. 82, No. 80

A Section–through composed

Allegro agitato

* Bring out LH finger 5 in measures 7–10.

In the Forest

Cornelius Gurlitt (1820–1901)
Op. 82, No. 65

A Section–through composed
Allegro non troppo

Sonatina in C Major

Op. 36, No. 1

This piece is from the

Muzio Clementi was an Italian composer and pianist. He was highly regarded as a pianist and participated in a famous keyboard contest with Mozart. This sonatina is one of his most-famous works.

Baroque Era ca. 1600–1750	Classical Era ca. 1750–1820	Romantic Era ca. 1790–1910	Contemporary Era ca. 1900–present

Muzio Clementi
(1752–1832)

II.

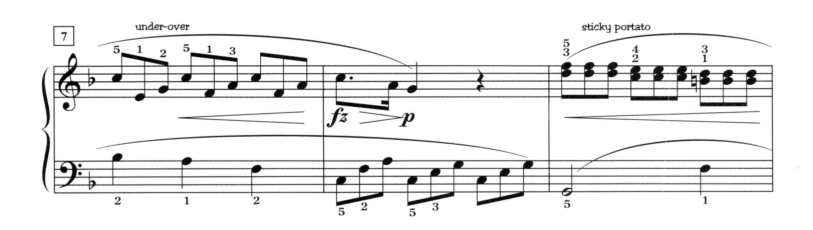

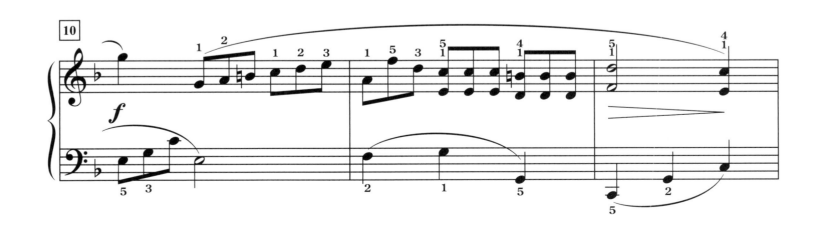

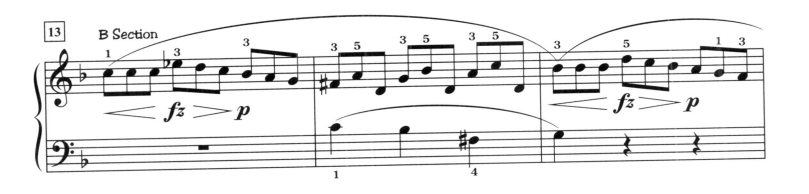

13 B Section

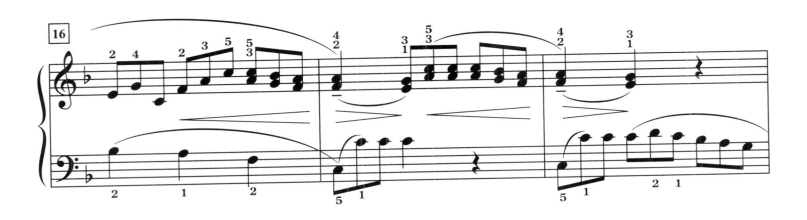

16

19 A¹ Section

23

arpeggio arch and pivot

34

III.

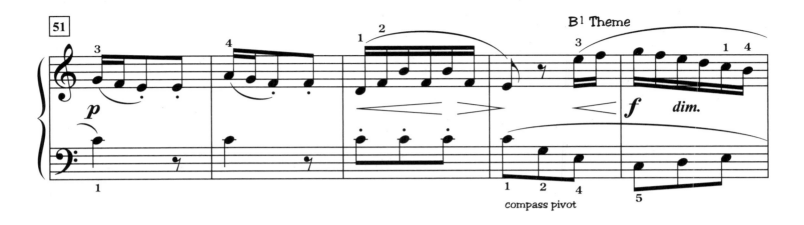

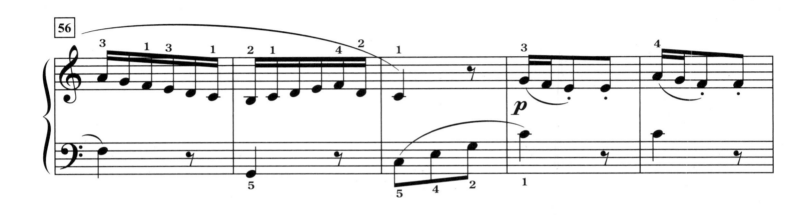

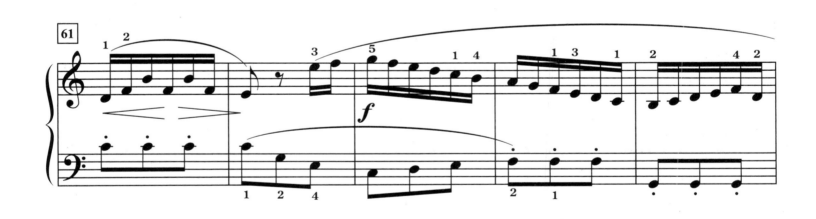

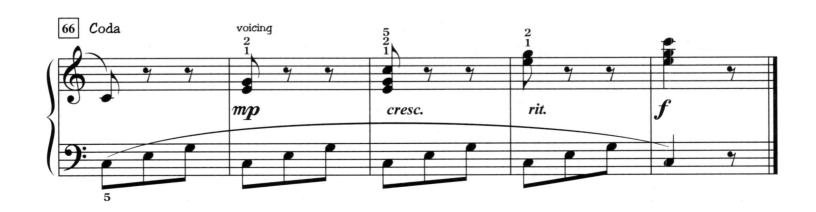

Waltz in A Minor

This piece is from the

Fritz Spindler was a German pianist and composer who was also well known as a teacher. He wrote many outstanding pedagogical works for pianists

| Baroque Era ca. 1600–1750 | Classical Era ca. 1750–1820 | Romantic Era ca. 1790–1910 | Contemporary Era ca. 1900–present |

Fritz Spindler
(1817–1905)

* In a waltz bass, use the elastic wrist on beat 1. Move the legato arm fluidly up to beat 2. On beats 2 and 3, play soft portatos with a minimum of arm weight.

Jeering Song
from *For Children*

This piece is from the

Béla Bartók wrote a well-known set of pieces called *For Children*. In these pieces, he captures a wide variety of emotions through many means including contrasting articulations and tempos.

Baroque Era ca. 1600–1750	Classical Era ca. 1750–1820	Romantic Era ca. 1790–1910	Contemporary Era ca. 1900–present

Béla Bartók
(1881–1945)

A¹ Section

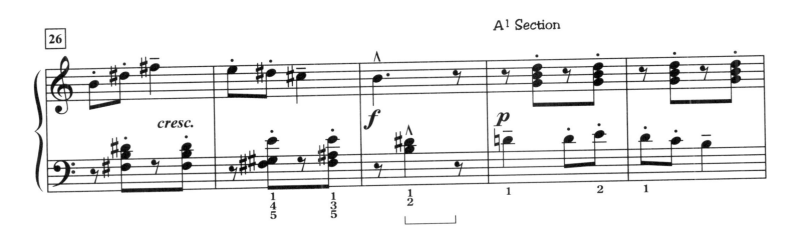

Coda

a tempo

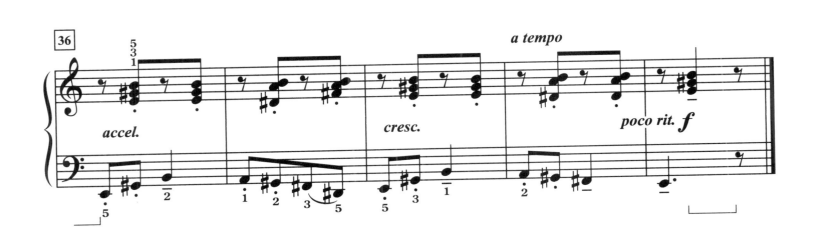

Allegro in B-flat Major
K. 3

This piece is from the

Wolfgang Amadeus Mozart was a brilliant Austrian composer. He was the greatest child prodigy, known as both a composer and keyboardist. As an adult, he fell upon hard times and died at age 35 in poverty.

| Baroque Era ca. 1600–1750 | Classical Era ca. 1750–1820 | Romantic Era ca. 1790–1910 | Contemporary Era ca. 1900–present |

Wolfgang Amadeus Mozart
(1756–1791)

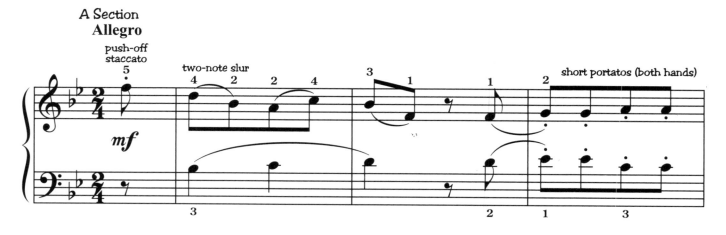

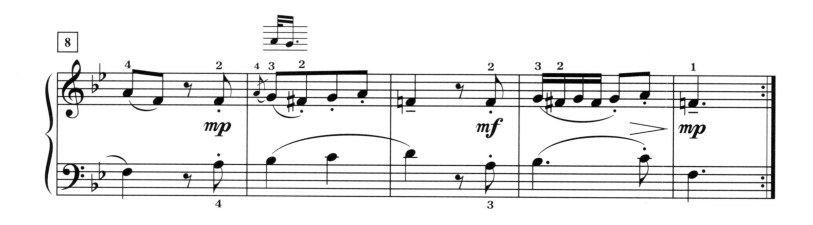

B Section

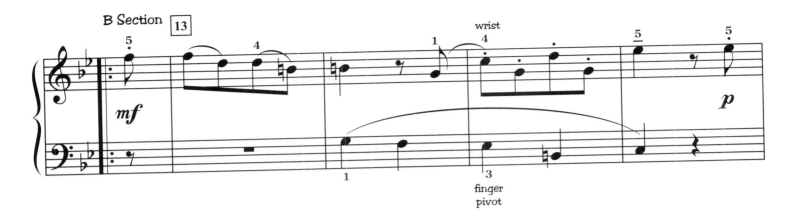

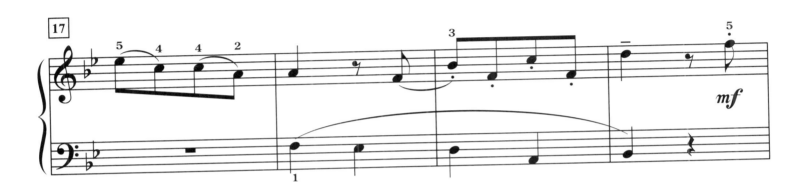

Bourrée in G Major

This piece is from the

George Frideric Handel was a German-born composer. As a young man, he moved to England. He became a British subject in 1727. He was well known for his oratorios, operas, and keyboard works.

| Baroque Era ca. 1600–1750 | Classical Era ca. 1750–1820 | Romantic Era ca. 1790–1910 | Contemporary Era ca. 1900–present |

George Frideric Handel
(1685–1759)

A Section
Allegretto

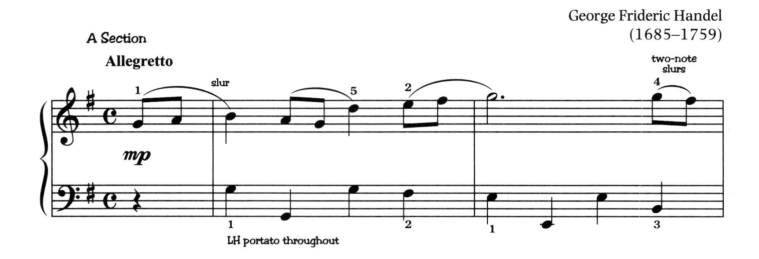

LH portato throughout

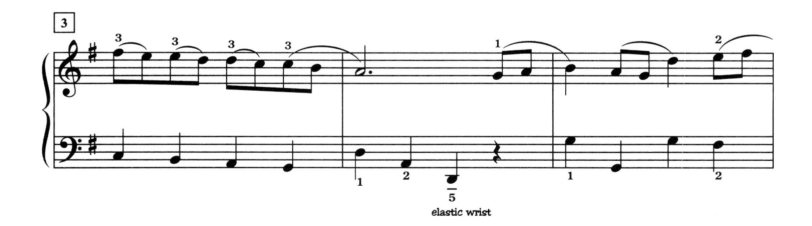

elastic wrist

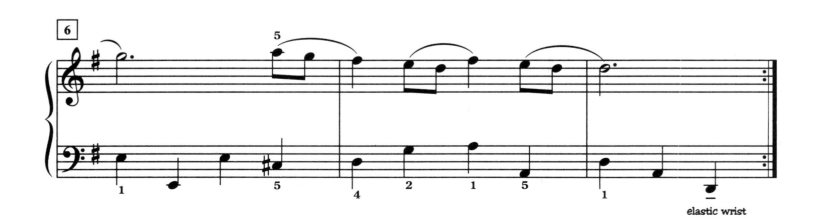

elastic wrist

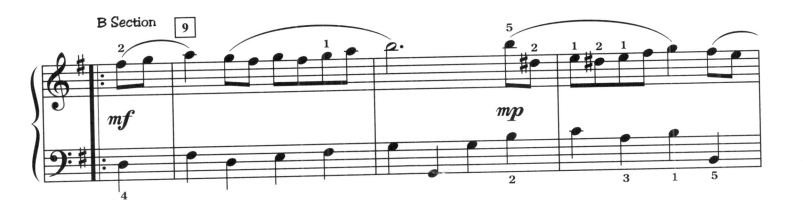

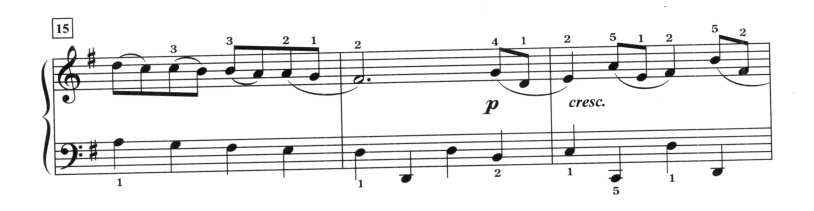

Scherzo in A Minor

This piece is from the

Carl Maria von Weber was a German composer, pianist, and conductor. He was best known for his operas. Although he lived in the Classical era, his compostitions often foreshadowed the Romantic era in their dramatic character.

| Baroque Era ca. 1600–1750 | Classical Era ca. 1750–1820 | Romantic Era ca. 1790–1910 | Contemporary Era ca. 1900–present |

Carl Maria von Weber
(1786–1826)

Sonatina in C Major

This piece is from the

Alexander Goedicke was a Russian composer, pianist, and teacher. He received the prestigious Rubenstein Prize for Composition at the age of 23. He is well known for his pedagogical piano music and his *Concert Etude* for trumpet.

| Baroque Era ca. 1600–1750 | Classical Era ca. 1750–1820 | Romantic Era ca. 1790–1910 | Contemporary Era ca. 1900–present |

A Theme—exposition

Allegro moderato (♩ = ca. 120)

Alexander Goedicke
(1877–1957)

A Theme–recapitulation

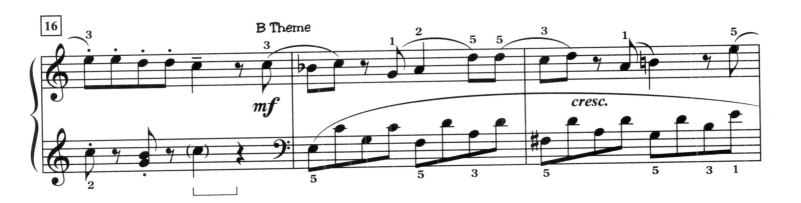

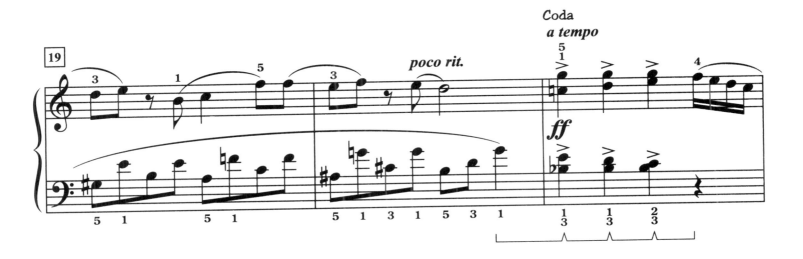

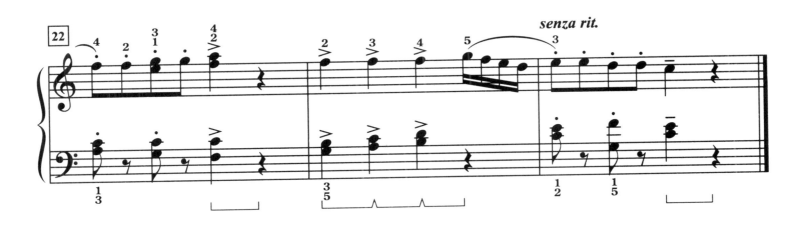

Technical Summary–Even Distribution of Arm Weight, One-Octave Arpeggio Skills and Six Advancing Technical Skills from Pathways to Artistry Technique Book 3

Even Distribution of Arm Weight

Compass Pivots

A. **Prepare and drop the arm weight**.

B. **Pivot and fluidly transfer weight to the primary pivotal center**.

C. **Continue pivoting** to the other side of the hand. (The wrist should draw an imaginary under-circle.)

Opening and Closing the Hand

A. **Drop** the arm weight.

B. **Pivot** on the playing finger as you **open the hand.**

C. When you are not playing with the thumb or fifth finger, **close them** and return to a relaxed, natural position.

One-Octave Arpeggio Skills

1. Arpeggio Pivots

A. **Drop the arm weight and pivot.**

B. **Open the hand and transfer the weight** to the next playing finger.

C. **Fluidly close the thumb or fifth finger** when they are not playing.

2. Balanced Arpeggios

A. **Align the hand and arm weight** with the playing finger.

B. **Lean the torso slightly** in the direction of the arpeggio.

C. **Follow** the direction of the arpeggio with the torso, arm and hand.

3. Arpeggio Arch

RH ascending to descending,
LH descending to ascending

A. **Drop the arm weight** into the first note.

B. **Combine** the fluid "under" motion of the **under-over wrist roll** with **arpeggio pivots** and **balanced arpeggios**.

C. Once you have reached the highest note of the right hand, or the lowest note of the left hand, **lift the wrist** and begin the **"arch over" motion.**

Arpeggio Arch

RH descending to ascending,
LH ascending to descending

A. **Drop the arm weight** into the first note.

B. **Lift the wrist** and **begin** the **"arch over."**

C. **Complete the "under" motion.**

Six Advancing Technical Skills

1. Alternating Hand Technique

A. **Analyze and practice the skills** for each individual hand.

B. **Practice and play** hands together **away** from the keyboard first.

C. **Return to the keyboard** and play hands together.

2. Chromatic Patterns and Scales

A. **Learn** the rules of chromatic fingering.

B. **As you play** each note, **simultaneously prepare** the hand for the next note.

C. **Keep the hand and arm at a slightly diagonal angle.**

3. Expanding and Contracting

A. **Expand** the hand at the moment of playing.

B. **Contract the hand immediately** after playing.

C. **Keep the hand** in a relaxed position until the next expansion.

4. Riding the Key

A. **Always keep** the finger or thumb that is riding the key in contact with the key.

B. **Use wrist rotation to throw** the weight to the keys that are not being "ridden."

C. **Feel adhered** to the key being "ridden."

5. Wrist Flips

A. **Adhere** the non-melodic thumb or finger to the key.

B. **Roll** the surface of the adhering thumb or finger slightly **away** from the flipping side.

C. With a fast motion, **combine** wrist rotation with **rolling back** on the adhering thumb or finger. This will create momentum to throw or **flip** the wrist and the weight of the arm and hand to the melodic notes.

6. Una Corda Pedal Technique

A. **Use the left foot as in damper pedal technique.**

B. **Prepare** to use the una corda and **engage only** as the artistic moment calls for it.

C. **Use your ear, depress before** the desired soft sound and **rehearse.**

* See *Pathways to Artistry Technique Book 3* for a comprehensive description of each skill. Other "physical vocabulary" skills in this book can be found in *Pathways to Artistry Technique Books 1 and 2*.